KILLER ANTS

by **Nicholas Nirgiotis**

illustrated by **Emma Stevenson**

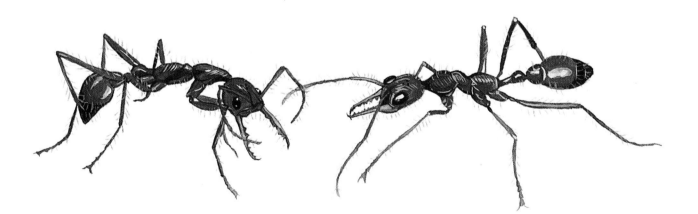

Holiday House / *New York*

Deep in a tropical forest,

a million soldiers are on the march. They hold their heads high. Their huge hooked jaws are wide-open. They are ready to do battle.

The soldiers are following a trail— marked by their scouts—toward a camp full of wild animals kept in cages while they wait to be sent to a zoo. Every step the soldiers take brings them closer and closer to the camp.

A watchman sits at the gate. But he is asleep. He cannot see the soldiers approaching. A bite on his leg makes him twitch. Immediately there is another bite on his arm.

The watchman's eyes snap open. He jumps up from his chair and slaps his neck. He slaps his arms and legs. "ARMY ANTS! ARMY ANTS!" he shouts.

There is no time to lose. The army ants are heading straight for the cages. The animals inside cannot run away. The watchman and the hunters who caught the animals are in an uproar. The whole camp is in confusion.

"Quick!" the watchman shouts. "Pile dry leaves and branches on the path. Soak the pile with kerosene. Then set it on fire."

It works. The ants in front feel the heat. They don't lose any time. They turn and run away. The others follow quickly. The ants have lost this battle. But they have survived, and they will hunt again tomorrow.

There are more than thirteen thousand species of ants. Each is a little different from all the others. Ants live almost everywhere—on mountainsides, in forests, in deserts, even in cities. Exceptions are Antarctica, Greenland, Iceland, and parts of Polynesia, plus remote islands in the Atlantic and Indian Oceans.

Leaf-cutters are farmers and gardeners. They cut pieces of leaves and carry them over their heads like umbrellas to their nests. The special fungus they grow on the leaf pulp is their only food.

Cattle-tending ants lick a sweet liquid called honeydew from the bodies of aphids and some scale insects.

Harvester ants gather seeds and store them in underground nests.

Honeypot ants store honey in the abdomens of special ants that hang from the ceiling of their nests like huge, fat jars.

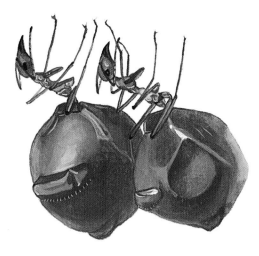

Other Ants Are Not So Peaceful

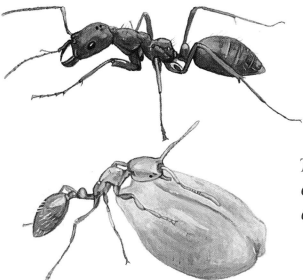

Red Amazons keep other ant species as slaves to do the work of finding food and caring for their young.

There's even a tiny ant that creeps into nests of bigger ants and steals their food.

The most dangerous of the tiny creatures are several species of flesh-eating killer ants. They swoop down on other insects or on animals much larger than they are. The ants bite their victims with their powerful jaws, tearing them to pieces, and often sting their prey in the process. Then they carry the pieces to their nests for food. These are the army ants that live in Central and South America and the driver ants of Africa. A few others, such as the red fire ants that live in the southern United States and the bulldog ants of Australia, are just as dangerous. In addition to their biting jaws, they too use venomous stingers to attack other animals and people who come near their nests.

Army Ants

Like all ants, army ants are social insects. They live in large colonies of hundreds of thousands, sometimes millions. But army ants differ from other ant species in many ways, including their biology. And unlike other ants, army ants do not build nests since they move from place to place often. Their temporary homes are called bivouacs.

Watching an army ant colony form its bivouac is like watching a circus performance. The ants make it with their own bodies. They gather under a fallen tree, in a hole in the ground, or between large rocks. The bivouac looks like a thick, rolled-up net made of layer upon layer of ants. Some people have compared it to a twitching jigsaw puzzle. The queen of the colony and her young are safe inside the bivouac.

The ants join together by holding on to one another with powerful hooked claws at the tips of their feet.

8

The queen is the mother of every ant in the colony. She lays many thousands of eggs every day. She must do so to keep the colony at full strength. The queen is four times larger than a worker ant. While she is in her egg-laying stage, the queen looks like a balloon. She is so heavy she cannot move out of the bivouac. The eggs she lays are precious, but the older juveniles, in which more has been invested, matter even more. Sometimes, when food is scarce, ants in the colony will eat the eggs to survive.

After an egg is laid, it develops into a wiggly larva that looks like a tiny white worm. Worker ants feed the larvae, which grow quickly. Each larva turns into a pupa that wraps itself in a homemade cocoon. A short time later, the ant inside opens the cocoon. Out pops a full-sized army ant ready for a life of hard work.

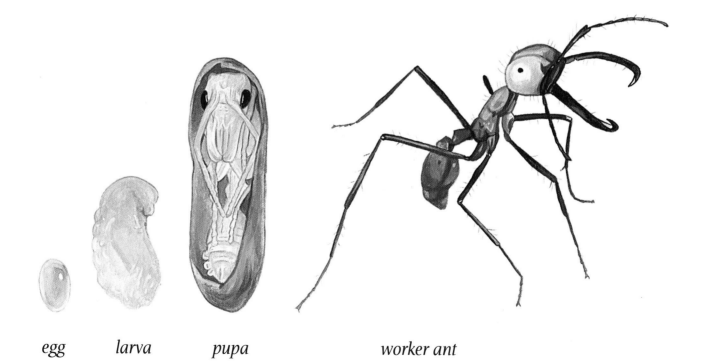

egg   *larva*   *pupa*
                    inside cocoon   *worker ant*

All the Workers in a Colony Are Female

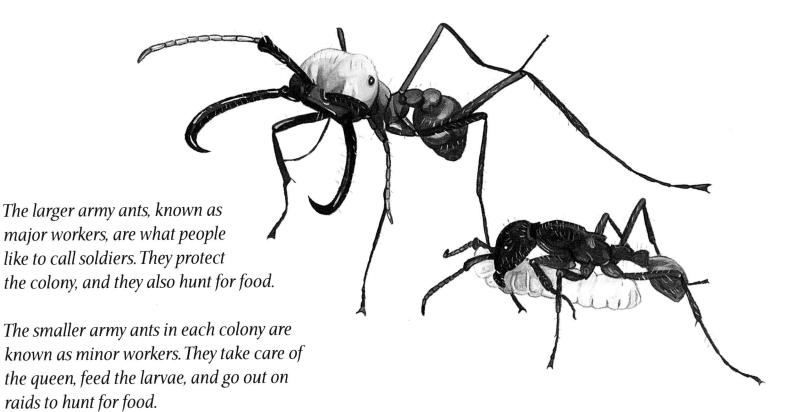

The larger army ants, known as major workers, are what people like to call soldiers. They protect the colony, and they also hunt for food.

The smaller army ants in each colony are known as minor workers. They take care of the queen, feed the larvae, and go out on raids to hunt for food.

Once a year in the dry season the queen gives birth to several young queens and about a thousand males. The males are the only ants in the colony with wings. The males never mate with the new queens in their own colony. They fly to other colonies to mate with the young queens there. After a short, happy life of mating, the males die. They live only two days. One of the new queens—but only one—will take a large number of workers and form her own colony. The other young queens soon die.

Army ants range in color and are about a half inch long, or as long as one of your fingernails.

The head is coconut shaped. Within it are the sense organs and a brain that some scientists believe is the most advanced in the insect world. To pull apart food, carry things, and fight, army ants use two strong, sickle-shaped jaws that open sideways on either side of the mouth.

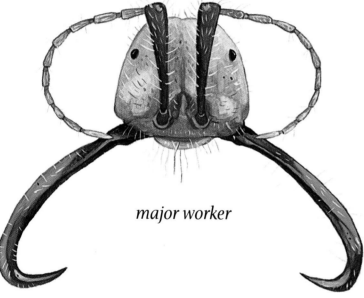

major worker

Minor workers have no eyes, and major workers' eyes are tiny. So the workers rely on their two antennae to know the world. They swivel and bend the antennae constantly. They touch other ants to recognize them or to pass and receive messages. The antennae "smell" the ground to pick up the scent other ants have left to warn of danger, tell where food is to be found, or point the way to the bivouac.

head

antenna

Like all insects, army ants have no bones inside their bodies. A hardened outer skin supports and protects their muscles and organs.

mandible, or jaw

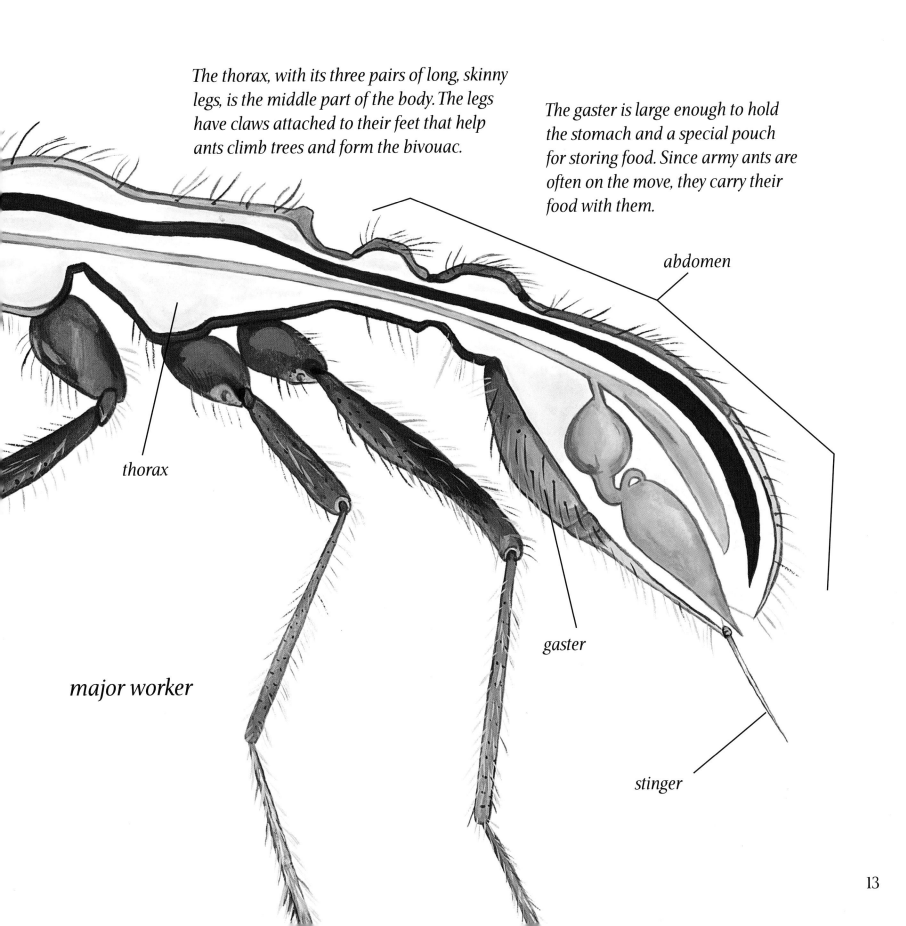

The thorax, with its three pairs of long, skinny legs, is the middle part of the body. The legs have claws attached to their feet that help ants climb trees and form the bivouac.

The gaster is large enough to hold the stomach and a special pouch for storing food. Since army ants are often on the move, they carry their food with them.

abdomen

thorax

major worker

gaster

stinger

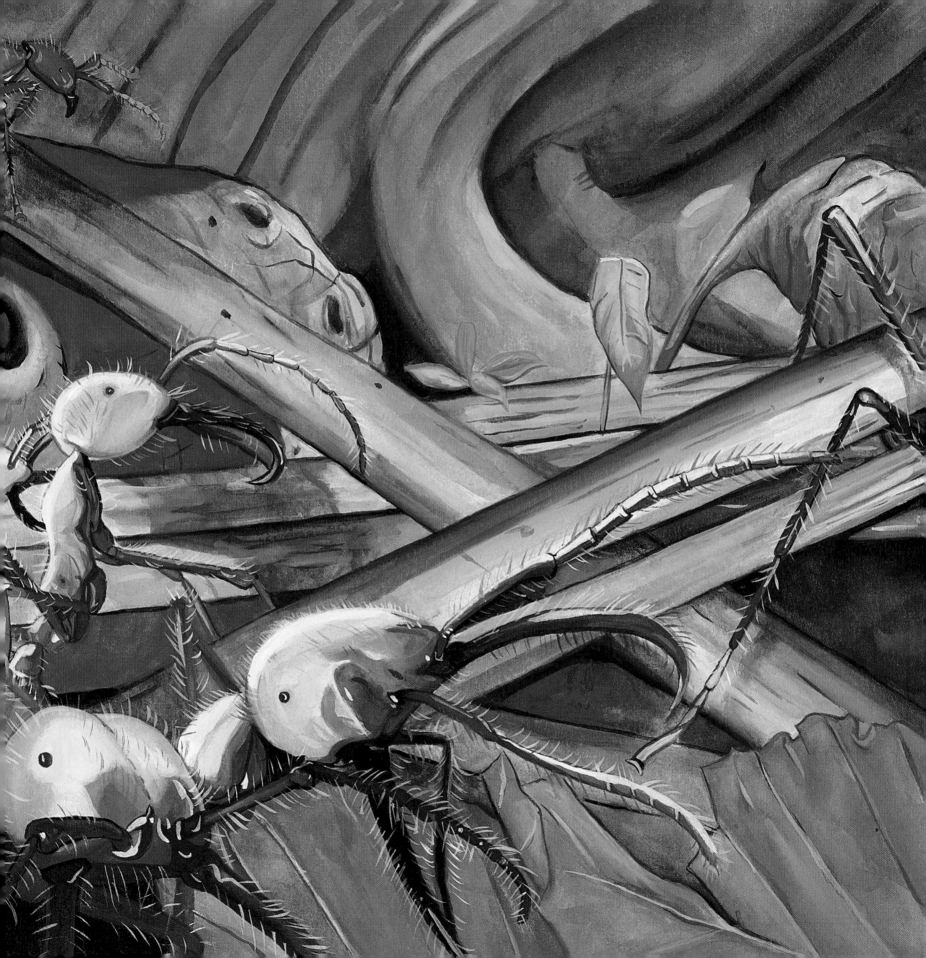

Different army ant species raid in different ways. A raid might happen like this: In the early morning light, tens of thousands of the ants let go of one another's feet. They pour out of the bivouac in a churning swarm. Soon the swarm forms into a single raiding column that can stretch as long as a football field and look like a moving stream of dark water.

Scouts go ahead to look for prey and lay down a chemical trail from a tiny opening at the tip of their abdomens. Some workers march on the outside to protect the column. Others are in the middle. The queen and the younger workers stay safely in the bivouac.

The column moves farther and farther into the forest. It climbs over logs and crosses gullies. It goes through leaf litter. Close to the prey it fans out like the branches of a tree.

No animal can fight a column of army ants because there are too many of them. Any creature in their path has to run for its life. The unlucky ones are caught. They squirm and try to escape. It's no use. If they are large, the workers sting them to subdue them. Then they rip them into small pieces with their powerful jaws and carry the booty of animal pieces to the bivouac to be eaten.

Army ants eat only invertebrates, which are animals with no backbones, such as other ants, spiders, scorpions, beetles, katydids, roaches, and grasshoppers. However, they will sting vertebrates, which are animals that have backbones, such as mice, frogs, nesting birds, small snakes, and lizards. They will even sting a large animal such as a deer or a pig too sick to run away or a large snake if it is too stuffed with food to move. Even human babies and old or handicapped people are in danger. Army ants are so ferocious people call them kings of the jungle.

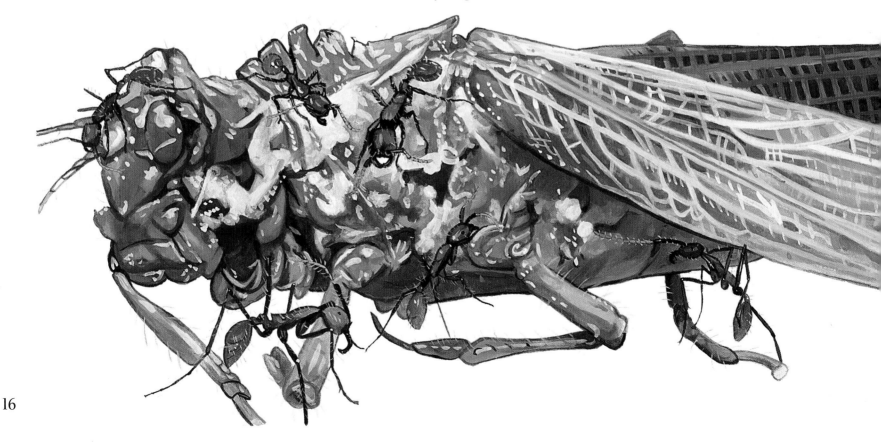

The colony stays in the same bivouac for two to three weeks. This is called the stationary period. The ants raid during the morning and retreat to the bivouac in the afternoon. The next morning they go out in a different direction. The queen lays her eggs and the larvae hatch. Young ants from the previous batch of eggs come out of their cocoons as adults. These new ants are restless and full of energy.

It is time to move the bivouac when the developing larvae need more food.

The queen lays her eggs.

The migratory stage lasts about two weeks. The column raids each day and moves during the night until a new location for the bivouac is found. There, the queen will start laying more eggs, and the cycle will begin again. She produces three hundred thousand eggs during each stationary phase and more than four million eggs in a month.

The queen is no longer laying eggs, so she is slimmer and she can move easily.

How brave are you? Could you let army ants crawl all over your body? Some indigenous tribes (such as Matis and Karamani) in the Amazon rain forest test young boys to see how brave they are. When they are twelve, the boys are left in a room full of army ants. The grown-ups wait to see how long it takes before the boys ask for help.

Driver Ants

African driver ants resemble the South American army ants with a few differences. Unlike army ants, they eat vertebrates and live in underground nests. Plus, they use their powerful jaws to cut up, rather than pull apart, their victims. But like army ants, they raid in such great numbers and their bites are so fierce that they "drive" before them every living thing that can move.

There is great excitement when a driver ant raid gets under way.

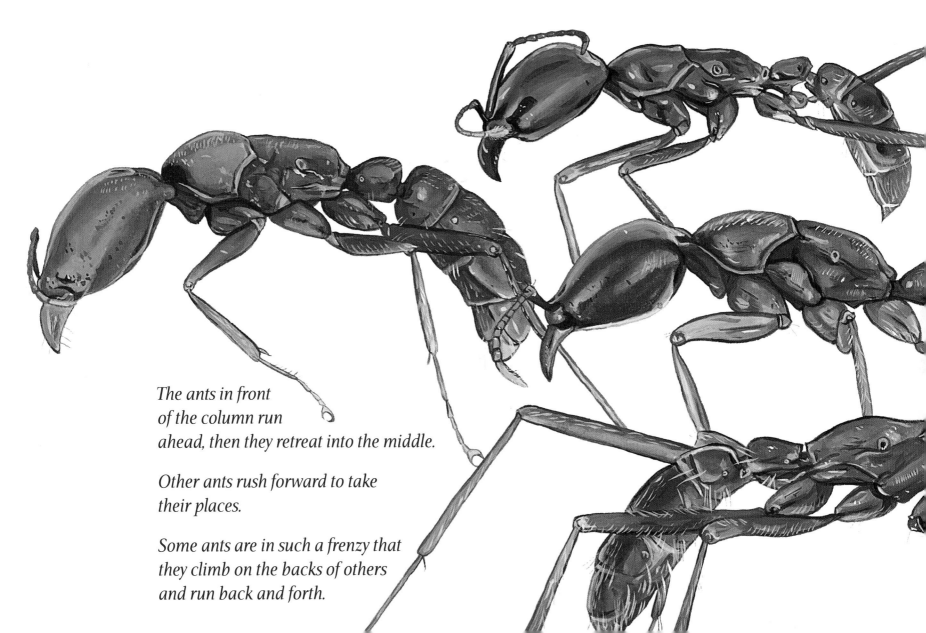

The ants in front of the column run ahead, then they retreat into the middle.

Other ants rush forward to take their places.

Some ants are in such a frenzy that they climb on the backs of others and run back and forth.

Despite this confusion, the raiding column moves forward about fifty feet an hour. That may seem slow, but the ants get where they want to go just the same.

There are many stories of driver ants attacking people. One is about the African explorer Dr. David Livingstone. One of his scariest adventures was when a column of the ants raided his camp. His helpers ran away, but Livingstone stayed in his tent. He could see driver ants everywhere. He lay still on his bed, thinking that the ants would not attack him. Why should they? He was not bothering them. He was wrong.

The ants began to bite his arms, his legs, his back, his chest. Blood oozed from the bites. Livingstone ran out of his tent and called for help. Luckily his men were close by. They lit fires to smoke the ants away, then they spent hours plucking ants off Livingstone's body.

Some Africans shiver with fear when they tell stories of how, long ago, some cruel kings used to punish criminals. Anyone convicted of murder or an equally serious crime was tied on the ground near a driver ant nest and left to be torn to pieces.

People who live in the rain forest, though, have a special use for driver ants. When they see a column approaching their village, they leave their homes. The ants march in and kill the roaches, mice, lizards, tarantulas, snakes, and all other pests that hide in the huts. Then they take the pieces back to their nest. When the people return, their homes are squeaky-clean. Driver ants are nature's best exterminators.

Fire Ants

Soon after Columbus reached the New World, Europeans came to live on many of the Caribbean islands. New towns sprang up in Hispaniola, Jamaica, Barbados, and Martinique. The colonists immediately ran into a problem. Fire ants had been living on the same islands long before the newcomers. The ants were not happy to share their home with them.

Great swarms of fire ants came into the homes of the colonists and crawled all over their bodies, biting and stinging. Many of the colonists became sick, and a few died. The problem was so bad the colonists were afraid they might have to leave their towns. They had no way of protecting themselves, so they prayed to their saints and asked God for help. In desperation, the governor of one of the islands offered thousands of gold pieces to anyone who could find a way to get rid of the dangerous pests. No one was able to win the prize. As time passed fire ants and colonists learned to live with each other.

Red fire ants did not live in the United States until 1918. That year ships unloading lumber from South America brought the ants to the port of Mobile, Alabama, by accident. Since they found no natural enemies and they liked the climate, the ants spread all across the southern states, from Florida to Texas.

As the fire ants moved westward, they displaced other species of ants living in those states. Today they are considered to be the number one pest in the United States, and efforts are being made to root them out—with little success. Fire ants live up to the name scientists have given one species, *Solenopsis invicta,* which means "the unbeatable ones."

Even though fire ants are about one-fifth of an inch long, they are so nasty and dangerous that they are called the ants from hell. What makes the ant dangerous is a needle-sharp stinger at the tip of the abdomen that it uses to inject venom into its victims. All those who have been stung say it feels as if someone has touched their skin with burning matches. Typically, many fire ants sting at one time, not just one ant.

An Attack by a Fire Ant Comes in Two Steps

First, the ant grabs the skin with its sharp jaws and lifts it up.

Then it whips its gaster under its body, jabs its stinger into the flesh of the victim, and releases the venom.

A pink blister grows quickly where a fire ant has jabbed its stinger. The blister gradually fills with pus, and it itches. If the person scratches the spot, the blister may become infected. Worse, some people are allergic to the ant's venom and have difficulty breathing. If stung, they may die unless they get medical attention quickly.

The sting of one ant can paralyze a caterpillar. Many ants stinging together can kill a squirrel or a farm animal. And each ant can sting many times.

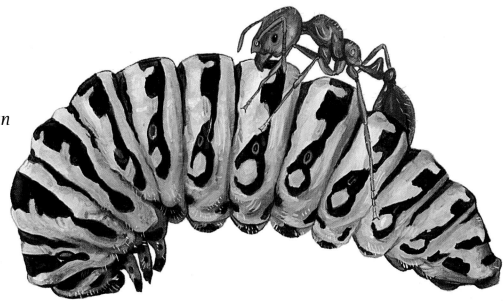

A fire ant colony can have 100,000 to 500,000 workers living in an underground nest. The nest is like a tall apartment building built upside down. Fire ants are skilled engineers. They build mounds over their nests from the soil brought up by the construction of the nest. The mounds, which can be up to two feet high, help control the temperature and the humidity inside. On cool mornings workers move the queen and the larvae near the top of the mound where the air is warmer. On hot days everyone moves deeper into the soil.

The nest has many chambers connected by tunnels to shelter the mother queen, the young, and the workers.

A few fire ants always stand guard at the entrance to the mound and use their antennae to check everyone that comes close. When a stranger that might be an enemy approaches, the guards release a chemical that brings thousands of their fellow workers rushing to the spot to bite and sting the intruder.

The nests are built in open, sunny fields; but they are also found in parks, in school yards, and around homes. Farmworkers and grazing animals, even children and pets, that come carelessly close to a nest are sure to be bitten and stung. These fiery little ants attack many thousands of people each year.

Unlike army ants, fire ants search for food singly; and they prefer corn, wheat, and soybean seeds. They often destroy growing plants by chewing on their stems and sucking the juices. Their favorite food is honeydew from aphids. But they will sometimes kill birds that have just hatched, as well as mice and insects, for food.

Although fire ants cannot swim, they have an unusual way of saving themselves from drowning in a flood. When the water rises, the entire colony gathers itself together. Each ant takes hold of another with the claws of its feet. The mass of ants floats on the water like a raft. To make sure ants underwater at the bottom have a chance to breathe, the mass rotates continually. When the ants touch solid ground, they dig a new nest and carry on with their lives as before.

Fire ants are sometimes helpful to humans. Ticks are a problem in some places because they spread Lyme disease, which sickens thousands of people every year. Fire ants kill ticks. As a result, many places where fire ants live will not have ticks. They also eat pests such as pecan weevils and sugarcane borers, which damage plants grown by farmers.

Bulldog Ants

Most of the animals that live in Australia are different from those that live anywhere else on Earth. That's true of ants too. Australia has a primitive species of ant called bulldog that can do something no other ant can do. Bulldog ants can jump up to seven times the length of their bodies. Australians call bulldog ants "jumpers" or "jack jumpers." Bulldog ants live in underground nests scattered beneath eucalyptus forests. Compared with those of other ants, their colonies are small.

Bulldog ants are mainly flesh eaters, and unlike other ants they prefer to hunt alone. They hide behind a rock or a clump of grass, leap at their victims, and sink saw-toothed jaws that look like pincers into their flesh. They were given their name for a good reason. Once they get a firm hold, they hang on like bulldogs. But it's the jab with the half-inch-long stinger and the venom it releases that kill the victim.

The last pair of its legs is strong enough to help it spring into the air like a grasshopper.

One of the largest ant species, bulldog ants grow as long as an inch. They look like wasps but without the wings. Their large bodies and large eyes set them apart from other ants.

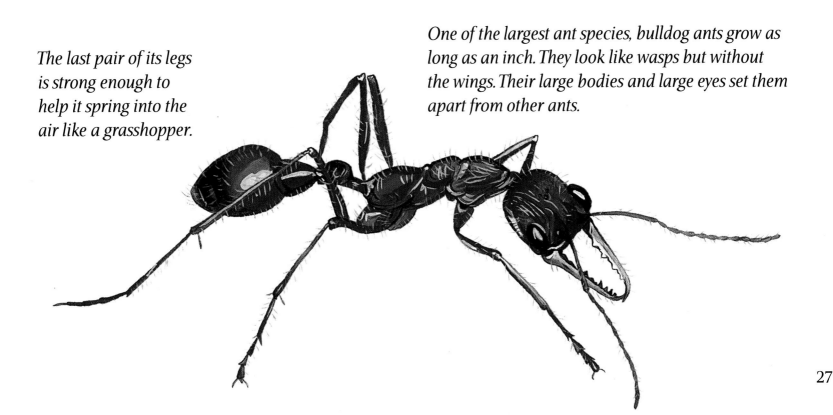

When a stranger comes close to their nest, bulldog ants swarm straight out, jaws open and stinger at the ready. Even a thick boot won't stop them. They simply jump over the boot to land on the victim's leg. The sting of a bulldog ant is so powerful that it sends waves of pain through the body that last for several days.

Can anything good come out of a fierce creature such as a bulldog ant? A clever doctor in New Guinea thought the ant's bite might be useful. Instead of closing a wound by stitching it together, he let the ants clamp their jaws around the opening. Then the bodies were removed before they could sting. A bulldog ant's grip is so firm, the jaws stayed on the flesh until the wound healed.

Do all these dangerous ants serve any useful purpose in nature? Are they here just to be nasty and mean to other animals and people? Myrmecologists are scientists who study ants. They tell us that if the vast number of insects and other small animals that army and driver ants devour each day were left unchecked, they would damage the rain forest. Killer ant raids help keep the forest clean and healthy.

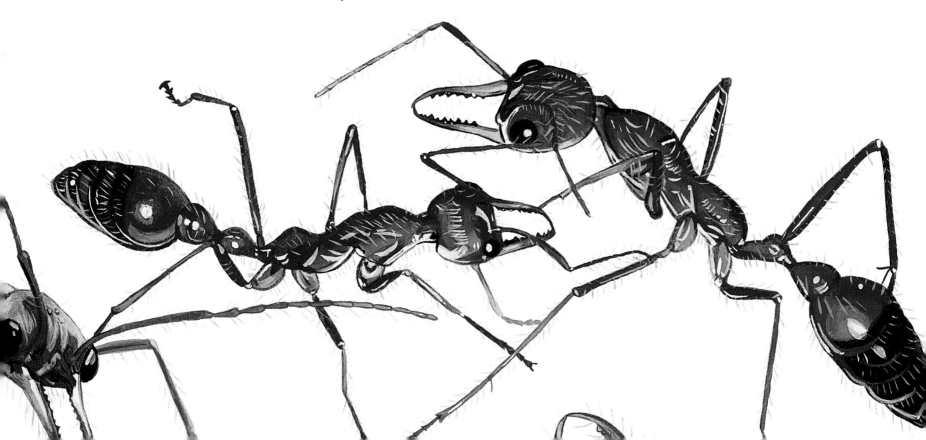

Ants Are One of Nature's Most Successful Life-Forms

Ants came into being more than a hundred million years ago, before the time of dinosaurs. Yet if you want to see one of the mighty dinosaurs, you have to go to a museum and look at a preserved skeleton.

All you have to do to see tiny ants going about their business is step out into your backyard.

Each year scientists report new discoveries about how ants and plants benefit each other. One example comes from Borneo, where a pitcher plant gets its food by trapping insects in a leaf-shaped cup filled with liquid. A certain species of ant nests inside the plant and feeds on excess prey that would disrupt the plant's digestive system. The ants help keep the plant healthy while using the plant as a food resource.

29

To Caitlin, Elena, and William. I love you in a special way. Your Papou —N. N.

To Mom, Dad, Richard, Rachael, and Gary —E.S.

Index

The publisher wishes to thank Louis Sorkin, entomologist at the American Museum of Natural History, for reviewing this book for accuracy.

Text copyright © 2009 by Nicholas Nirgiotis
Illustrations copyright © 2009 by Emma Stevenson
All Rights Reserved
HOLIDAY HOUSE is registered in the U.S. Patent and Trademark Office.
Printed and Bound in China
The text typeface is Veritas.
The artwork was created with layers of gouache on watercolor paper.
www.holidayhouse.com
First Edition
1 3 5 7 9 10 8 6 4 2
Library of Congress Cataloging-in-Publication Data
Nirgiotis, Nicholas. • Killer ants / by Nicholas Nirgiotis ; illustrated by Emma Stevenson. — 1st ed. • p. cm. • ISBN-13: 978-0-8234-2034-6 • (hardcover) •
1. Ants—Juvenile literature. 2. Predatory insects—Juvenile literature. I. Stevenson, Emma. II. Title. • QL568.F7N57 2009 • 595.79'6—dc22 • 2007046922